MW01155746

Plato
CHARMIDES

Plato

CHARMIDES

Translated by
THOMAS G. WEST and
GRACE STARRY WEST

HACKETT PUBLISHING COMPANY

Plato: *ca* 428-347 B.C.

Copyright © 1986 by Hackett Publishing Company
All rights reserved
Printed in the United States of America

06 05 04 03 02 01 00   3 4 5 6 7 8 9

Interior design by J. M. Matthew

For further information, please address

    Hackett Publishing Company, Inc.
    P.O. Box 44937
    Indianapolis, Indiana 46244-0937

Library of Congress Cataloging in Publication Data

Plato.
    Charmides

    Bibliography: p.
    1. Ethics, Greek—Early works to 1800. 2. Knowledge,
Theory of —Early works to 1800. I. West, Thomas G.,
1945-　. II. West, Grace Starry, 1946-
III. Title
B366.A5W47 1986   184   85-24934
ISBN 0-87220-010-8 (pbk.)

The paper used in this publication meets the minimum
requirements on American National Standard for
Information Sciences—Permanence of Paper for Printed
Library Materials, ANSI Z39.48-1984

∞

Contents

Acknowledgments

WE WISH to thank the Earhart Foundation for a grant that enabled us to undertake this project.

The introduction and most of the interpretive notes to the translation are substantially indebted to several of David L. Levine's papers and articles on the dialogue, and especially to his "Plato's *Charmides*: On the Political and Philosophical Significance of Ignorance" (Ph.D. dissertation, Pennsylvania State University, 1975). Professor Levine gets to the heart of what the *Charmides* is about better than any scholar we have read. We have also followed his textual suggestions in several instances, notably at translation notes 15 and 23. Finally, Professor Levine suggested several items for the bibliography.

Thanks also to Hackett's two readers for their sharp but helpful criticisms, to Cecilia Rodriguez, who typed the whole manuscript, and to Carnes Lord, who originally suggested that we translate the *Charmides* for a collection he intended to edit.

We welcome suggestions for improving the translation. Comments can be addressed to us in care of our publisher.

University of Dallas   T.G.W.
                                                       G.S.W.

Introduction

Note on the Translation.

OUR AIM is a closely accurate English rendition of the Greek. We translate word for word wherever possible, and we follow as best as we can the sentence structure of the Greek. In the most important cases, we try to use a single English word for each recurrent Greek one. Reading such a text takes getting used to. But we hope that our translation allows the simplicity and vigor of the Greek diction to shine through the English. This version of the *Charmides* is intended to be at once more reliable and more vivid than other available translations.

The *Charmides* was translated from Burnet's Oxford edition of the Greek text (see Selected Bibliography). We have followed the manuscript readings in some cases where Burnet changes them. These departures are mentioned in the notes when they oeem important.

We have used paragraph divisions and quotation marks in the translation and have divided the dialogue into sections. There were no such divisions or devices in the original.

Setting and Characters

NO ONE knows when Plato wrote the *Charmides*. Most scholars believe it to be an early dialogue, composed not long after Socrates' death in 399 B.C.

The *Charmides* is set in Athens just after the siege and battle of Potidaea (431 B.C.), the first important engagement of

1

the long Peloponnesian War between Athens and Sparta. At the time of the dialogue Socrates, a relatively young man of thirty-eight, has just returned from the battle.

Socrates narrates the dialogue to a nameless companion who seems unaware that there had been a battle at Potidaea. Perhaps Socrates is telling the story of his first encounter with Charmides to a young man some years later.

The principal characters with whom Socrates converses are Charmides and Critias. Although Charmides is probably no older than eighteen, he dominates the first part of the dialogue through his charm and extraordinary beauty. The conclusion of the dialogue anticipates Charmides' later association with Socrates, about which we know little from the works of Plato. Charmides is mentioned briefly in the *Protagoras* (315a) and *Theages* (128e). More significant is Alcibiades' assertion, at the end of his drunken speech in the *Symposium,* that Socrates deceived Charmides into supposing that he was Charmides' lover while in fact making himself more Charmides' beloved than lover (222b).

We learn something more about Socrates' later dealings with Charmides from Xenophon. According to this author Socrates had a high opinion of Charmides' political abilities; he encouraged him to overcome his undue respectfulness toward the Assembly and become active in Athenian politics (*Memorabilia* III 7). In his *Symposium* Xenophon portrays Charmides as a companion of Socrates.

In the latter part of the *Charmides* Socrates converses at length with Charmides' uncle and guardian Critias, who had been an associate of Socrates before the war (156a). In his *Timaeus* and *Critias* Plato shows Critias to be on good terms with Socrates many years later. Elsewhere in Plato, Critias appears only in the *Protagoras* (316a and 336d). Critias held a certain reputation in antiquity for his poetry, some fragments of which have survived.[1] But he is most famous, or rather notorious,

---

1. *The Older Sophists,* ed. Rosamond Kent Sprague (Columbia: University of South Carolina Press, 1972), pp. 241–270, contains these fragments and also reports information from antiquity about Critias' life and work.

for his political activity, which culminated in his leading role in the oligarchy that ruled Athens after its defeat in the Peloponnesian War, twenty-seven years after the dialogue in the *Charmides*. Critias became "the most rapacious and violent and murderous"[2] of the "Thirty Tyrants," whose harsh regime terrorized Athens during their brief six-month reign. Charmides, as one of the "Ten in the Piraeus" installed by the Thirty, was one of Critias' leading collaborators. Each man died a violent death in separate battles with the supporters of the democracy. Both men, incidentally, were relatives of Plato.[3]

The overthrow of the Thirty in 403 preceded by four years Socrates' trial for impiety and corrupting the youth. According to Xenophon, Socrates' alleged corruption of Critias was a leading concern of his prosecutors (*Memorabilia* I 2.12-48). The present dialogue may be taken as part of Plato's defense of Socrates against this charge.

One character, Chaerephon, has a brief part at the beginning of the dialogue. Chaerephon was the man who, according to Socrates, asked the Delphic oracle if there was anyone wiser than Socrates (*Apology of Socrates* 21a). Chaerephon also appears at the beginning of the *Gorgias* and as Socrates' principal companion in a comedy, Aristophanes' *Clouds*.

The Drama and the Argument

THE OPENING PAGES of the dialogue describe a playful conspiracy between Socrates and Critias to strip and contemplate the soul of the beautiful Charmides. The rest of the dialogue is mainly a conversation, first between Socrates and Charmides, then Socrates and Critias, about what *sōphrosynē* is. The Greek word covers a range of English meanings, from "moderation" to

---

2. The phrase is from Xenophon, *Memorabilia* I 2.12.

3. The history of the Thirty is told in Xenophon, *Hellenica* II 3-4. Charmides was Plato's uncle, the brother of his mother Perictione.

"sound-mindedness." Thus in typically Platonic fashion the *Charmides* investigates a "what is——?" question by embedding it in a personal drama.

The notes to the translation explain some of the twists and turns of the arguments about moderation/sound-mindedness. We will not attempt to go beyond those notes here. Readers are directed to the Selected Bibliography for more thorough scholarly treatments.

But a word may be appropriate about how the action of the dialogue affects the argument. Charmides and Critias both have high opinions of themselves. Yet by the dialogue's end neither has been able to explain what sound-mindedness is. Nor has Socrates, to be sure. But throughout the discussion Socrates recognizes his own ignorance and tries to remedy it, while Charmides and Critias seem satisfied to be just as they are. Charmides' beauty and charm dazzle everyone around him, and he is tempted to believe the extravagant praises bestowed on him. Critias is highly renowned for his wisdom and cleverness. Socrates makes much of the cousins' aristocratic family background. Only at the end, when Charmides promises to become a follower of Socrates, does he show some awareness of being in need. This theme of *need* pervades the *Charmides*.

In the latter part of the dialogue Socrates and Critias investigate the view that sound-mindedness is a knowledge of knowledge and of non-knowledge—a kind of knowledge that enables one to recognize oneself and others, that is, to know what one knows and what one doesn't know—that one doesn't know it. Although the *argument* does not establish that such a knowledge exists, the *drama* shows Socrates to be in possession of that knowledge and recognition, for he frankly acknowledges his own ignorance—his *need* for the knowledge he lacks—even as he capably exposes the lacks of Critias and Charmides. The two cousins' sense of shame—their fear of disgracing themselves in the eyes of others—prevents them from admitting their deficiency, even to themselves, and they are thereby prevented from knowing themselves.

Since Plato chose to make two future tyrants discuss moderation/sound-mindedness with Socrates in the dialogue on the subject, we may infer some connection between their lack of sound-mindedness in the precise sense discussed in the dialogue—knowledge of knowledge and of ignorance—and their lack of moderation in the ordinary sense of self-restraint and "nothing too much." Critias in particular seems to believe that he knows all he needs to know, including what is good for himself and others. He therefore very much likes Socrates' vision of a technocratic utopia managed by knowers of knowledge who make sure everything is done by experts (171d–172c). It seems that Critias suffers from the tyrannical temptation that occurs precisely when one sees no limit to one's own knowledge and consequently undertakes to turn the world upside down for the sake of absolute perfection.[4] (In this respect his attitude foreshadows that of Stalin as portrayed by Solzhenitsyn in *The First Circle*.) Critias is certainly different from the crudely erotic tyrant of *Republic* Books 8 and 9, whose passion is limited to hedonistic self-indulgence.

The rival accounts of sound-mindedness discussed by Socrates and Critias point to the alternative ways of life of the philosopher and the tyrant. The contest between philosophy and tyranny, the great theme of *Republic* Book 9, is repeated in a subtler but perhaps more precise way in the *Charmides*. In the *Apology of Socrates* the philosopher tells the jury that "he knows that he does not know" about the most important things. In the *Charmides* we see Socrates' account of this knowledge of non-knowledge. We see it partly through Critias' presentation of what seem to be distorted versions of Socratic arguments. We also hear Socrates' own account of sound-mindedness presented unobtrusively through his occasional remarks and clarifications as the dialogue proceeds.

The life of examining oneself and others made possible by Socratic moderation/sound-mindedness is modest and ardu-

4. Some such concern may have originally animated the Thirty: Plato, *Seventh Letter* 324c–d.

ous and may even appear somewhat ugly. Critias obviously prefers the brilliance, however illusory, of the utopia sketched but rejected by Socrates. Even Socrates does not call moderation/sound-mindedness a virtue (*aretē*) in this dialogue. Still, it appears to be the *condition* of genuine virtue, the solid ground in which human greatness must take root if it is to thrive and not fester.

Sound-Mindedness

A MAJOR THEME of the dialogue is the meaning of *sōphrosynē*, here translated "sound-mindedness" throughout. As we have observed, this elusive term ranges in meaning from "moderation" to "self-control" to "discretion" and even "prudence." *Sōphrosynē* is composed of the roots *sō* ("sound," "safe," "saving"), and *phro-* ("mind," "thought," "sense," "heart"). No single English expression captures it. We used "moderation" in *Four Texts on Socrates: Plato's Euthyphro, Apology, and Crito, and Aristophanes' Clouds* (Ithaca: Cornell University Press, 1984). But "moderation" will not do for the *Charmides*, where the speakers particularly investigate the "mindful" aspect of "sound-mindedness."

The several meanings of moderation/sound-mindedness discussed in the *Charmides* are listed in the outline that follows this Introduction. The three definitions proposed by Charmides describe the stages through which all must pass, it seems, to become sound-minded. The very young are told to "keep quiet," "keep still." At that age "moderation" is imposed by parental restraint of external conduct. When children become a bit older, they hear, "you should be ashamed of yourself." These children develop within themselves a fear of disgracing themselves and a respect for the standards of conduct taught by their elders. Finally, adult sound-mindedness must be grounded on a right judgment of "one's own things"— of what is suitable for a given person to do in a given setting. But what are "one's own things"? This is the difficult question pursued by Critias and Socrates in the latter part of the dialogue.

Remarkably, no one in the *Charmides* proposes the most obvious definition of moderation/sound-mindedness: self-control, especially rule over the bodily passions for drink, sex, and food (as in *Republic* 389e, *Symposium* 196c, and the thematic account in Aristotle's *Nicomachean Ethics*, Book 3). It seems that the *Charmides* deliberately looks away from this popular sort of moderation toward the kind that is meant when one solemnly forces the equation of prudence with moderation/sound-mindedness (*Laws* 710a). We may compare the *Republic*, which nowhere discusses the obvious and popular definition of justice: obeying the laws. In each case the intention is to unearth the deepest meaning of the thing in question.

Other important Platonic discussions of moderation/sound-mindedness are *Gorgias* 503d–508c, *Republic* 430e–432a, and *Statesman* 309a–end.

Outline of the Charmides

WHILE READING the *Charmides* it is sometimes easy to get lost in the argument, particularly in the long discussion between Socrates and Critias. We therefore offer the following outline of the order of the argument.

161b   3. Third: *doing one's own things*—a definition Charmides heard from Critias. But what can "doing one's
own things" mean?

III.   Socrates and Critias discuss sound-mindedness.[5]

162c   1. Critias explains: doing one's own things means doing
what is beneficial and beautiful. He cites Hesiod.

163d   2. Socrates reformulates: sound-mindedness is the *doing
of good things*. But Critias agrees that one must also
recognize whether one is benefiting oneself, so he
redefines it: *oneself recognizing oneself*. Prompted by
Socrates, he restates it yet again: *a knowledge of itself
and of the other knowledges*. Socrates reformulates: *a
knowledge of knowledge and of non-knowledge*.

3. Is such a knowledge possible? And if possible, is it
beneficial?

167b   (1) A knowledge directed at itself seems strange in
light of the difficulty or impossibility of other
self-relations (a seeing that sees itself, etc.).

169d   (2) Assuming such a knowledge is possible, is it
beneficial? It seems not, because one who has a
knowledge of knowledge and of non-knowledge
knows only *that* he knows and doesn't know, not
what he knows and doesn't know. (This knowledge cannot recognize a real or fake doctor, only
that someone knows or doesn't know something
or other.)

171d   (3) Would it be beneficial even if one *could* recognize
what one knows and doesn't know? It seems not,
because it cannot be beneficial unless it knows
good and bad.

175a   Conclusion: Socrates sums up the perplexities of the argument.
Charmides obeys Critias and is ready to become a follower of
Socrates, by violence if necessary.

5. The two major hinges on which the long Critias section turns are the "new
beginnings" indicated by Socrates at 163d and 167b when he uses the expression
"back again...from the beginning."

Selected Bibliography

The Greek Text

Burnet, John, ed. *Platonis Opera*, vol. 3. Oxford Classical Texts. Oxford: Clarendon Press, 1903.

Croiset, Alfred, ed. *Hippias Majeur, Charmide, Lachès, Lysis*. Vol. 2 of *Platon: Oeuvres Complètes*. Paris: Société d'Edition "Les Belles Lettres," 1965.

On the Charmides

The items listed here represent the best recent writings in English on the *Charmides*. The selections include several quite different approaches, as indicated in the comments. One German book is mentioned to indicate the orientation of continental European scholarship toward the dialogue.

Bruell, Christopher. "Socratic Politics and Self-Knowledge: An Interpretation of Plato's *Charmides*." *Interpretation* 6 (1977): 141–203. A detailed and careful discussion by a student of Leo Strauss.

Dyson, M. "Some Problems Concerning Knowledge in Plato's *Charmides*." *Phronesis* 19 (1974): 102–111.

Friedländer, Paul. *Plato*, vol. 2: *The Dialogues, First Period*, pp. 67–81. Trans. Hans Meyerhoff. New York: Pantheon, 1964.

Guthrie, W.K.C. *A History of Greek Philosophy*, vol. 4: *Plato: The Man and His Dialogues, Earlier Period*, pp. 155–174. Cambridge: Cambridge University Press, 1975. Guthrie and Friedländer are standard treatments by classicists.

Hyland, Drew. *The Virtue of Philosophy: An Interpretation of Plato's Charmides.* Athens: Ohio University Press, 1981. An existential reading.

Klein, Jacob. *A Commentary on Plato's Meno.* Chapel Hill: University of North Carolina Press, 1965. The fine introduction on how to read Plato contains a seven-page discussion of knowledge of non-knowledge in the *Charmides.*

Levine, David L. "The Tyranny of Scholarship." *Ancient Philosophy* 4 (1984): 65-72. A substantial essay on the *Charmides,* with a critique of Hyland's book. The introduction and many of the notes to our translation are substantially indebted to Levine's "Plato's *Charmides*" (Ph.D. dissertation, Pennsylvania State University, 1975). Levine's new book on the dialogue is forthcoming.

Martens, Ekkehard. *Das selbstbezügliche Wissen in Platos Charmides* ("Self-Related Knowledge in Plato's *Charmides*"). Munich: Karl Hanser, 1973. The most important European book on the dialogue.

Rosen, Stanley. "Self-Consciousness and Self-Knowledge in Plato and Hegel." *Hegel-Studien* 9 (1974): 109-129.

———."*Sōphrosynē and Selbstbewusstsein.*" *Review of Metaphysics* 32 (1973): 617-642. Rosen's two articles compare the modern idea of self-consciousness with ancient self-knowledge.

Santas, Gerasimos X. "Socrates at Work on Virtue and Knowledge in Plato's *Charmides.*" In *Exegesis and Argument: Studies in Greek Philosophy Presented to Gregory Vlastos.* Ed. E.N. Lee, et al. *Phronesis* suppl. vol. 1, pp. 105-32. Assen: Van Gorcum, 1973. Santas, like Dyson and Wellman, uses the analytic approach.

Sprague, Rosamond Kent, trans. Plato. *Laches and Charmides*. Indianapolis: Hackett, 1992. Contains a translation with notes.

———. *Plato's Philosopher-King: A Study of the Theoretical Background*, pp. 29–42. Columbia: University of South Carolina Press, 1976. A recent study by a classicist.

Tuckey, T.G. *Plato's Charmides*. Cambridge Classical Studies, 1951; repr., Amsterdam: Hakkert, 1968. The only book-length study by a classicist.

Wellman, Robert R. "The Question Posed at *Charmides* 165a–165c." *Phronesis* 9 (1964): 107–113.

CHARMIDES

[Or, On Sound-Mindedness][1]

We came on the day before in the evening from Potidaea,[2]   153a
from the army camp, and because I had arrived after some
time away, I gladly went around to the places where I usually
spend my time. In particular I went to the wrestling school of
Taureas, the one right across from the temple of the Queen.[3]
And I found very many people there, some, to be sure, whom I
didn't recognize, but most of them acquaintances. And as they
saw me entering unexpectedly, they greeted me right away   b
from afar, one from one place, another from another.

But Chaerephon, that madman, leapt up from their

1. The subtitle may have been Plato's, or, more likely, it may have been added
by a later Greek editor. On the translation of sōphrosynē as sound-mindedness,
see the Introduction.

2. In one of the opening hostilities of the Peloponnesian War, Potidaea
revolted from its alliance with Athens, which besieged it for over a year at great
expense, forcing its surrender in 431 (Thucydides I 56–65, II 58, 70). In Plato's
Symposium Alcibiades praises Socrates' courage and endurance of hunger and
cold at Potidaea, where Socrates also saved Alcibiades' life when he was
wounded in battle (219e–220e).

Elsewhere in these notes, when works are mentioned without an author, they
are by Plato.

3. Nothing definite is known of this Taureas. "The Queen" (*Basilē*) may be a
goddess worshipped along with Codrus, a legendary early king of Athens and
supposed ancestor of Plato, Charmides, and Critias; or she may be Persephone,
the wife of Pluto-Hades, ruler of the underworld.

13

midst and ran to me, and taking me by the hand, said, "Socrates, how did you survive the battle?"

A little while before we had departed, a battle had occurred at Potidaea, which those here had just been learning about.

And I, answering him, said, "Just so, as you see."

"And yet it has been reported here," he said, "that the
c battle was quite fierce and that many of our acquaintances died in it."

"And what has been reported," I said, "is true enough."

"Were you present," he said, "at the battle?"

"I was present."

"Come here, then," he said; "sit down and go through it for us, for in fact we haven't yet found out everything plainly." And meanwhile he was leading me over and having me sit next to Critias, son of Callaeschrus.

So I sat down next to Critias and greeted him and the others, and I related the news of the army camp for them,
d whatever anyone asked me. One asked one thing, another asked another.

When we had enough of such things, I in turn asked them about the news here: about philosophy, how things stood with it, and about the young, whether any among them had become distinguished for wisdom or beauty or both. And
154a Critias looked toward the door, and seeing some youths entering and taunting one another, and another crowd following behind, said, "About the beautiful ones 4 Socrates, in my opinion you will know very soon. For those entering happen to be heralds and lovers of the one who is reputed to be the

---

4. "Beautiful" is usually used to translate *kalon*, a word of crucial importance in the *Charmides*. It can also mean "noble" or "fine," or in this context, "handsome." The word *kalon* suggests the splendid brilliance of something that shines forth, with the capacity for illumination as well as deception. In this text, we consistently use the translation "beautiful" even where other renderings would be more idiomatic so that the reader can follow the use of *kalon*.

most beautiful, right now, at least; and it appears to me that he
himself is approaching, probably already near."

"Who and whose son is he?⁵ I said.

"You know him, no doubt," he said, "but he wasn't yet
mature when you went away: Charmides, the son of our uncle   b
Glaucon, and my cousin."

"I certainly do know him, by Zeus!" I said; "for he was
in no way ordinary even then, when he was still a boy; and by
now I suppose he must be quite a lad."

"Very soon," he said, "you will know how mature he is
and what sort of person he has become." And as he was
saying this, Charmides entered.

Now nothing is to be measured by me, comrade, for I
am simply a white line⁶ when it comes to those who are
beautiful, because almost all who have just reached maturity
appear beautiful to me. But especially then he appeared
wondrous to me in both stature and beauty, and indeed, at   c
least in my opinion, all the others were in love with him, so
excited and confused had they become as he came in. Indeed,
many other lovers were also following among those behind
him. Now this was not wondrous on the part of us men; but
turning my attention to the boys, I noticed that none of them,
not even the littlest, looked anywhere else, but all were
contemplating him as if he were a statue.

And Chaerephon called to me and said, "How does the   d
youth appear to you, Socrates? Is he not fair of face?"

"Preternaturally so," I said.

"But if he should be willing to strip," he said, "he will

---

5. Literally, "Who and whose [or "of what"] is he?" This question points to a
major theme of the dialogue: Who is Charmides (he is to be "stripped" and
observed, 154e) and who or what is responsible for his being such as he is?

6. Literally, "white measure." This is a proverbial expression taken from
stonecutter's idiom. The mason used a line rubbed with chalk to mark the stones.
On white marble, a white chalk mark would be barely visible. "Simply" in this
sentence translates atechnōs, literally, "without skill or art."

seem to you to be faceless, so altogether beautiful is he in his looks."[7]

The others said the same as Chaerephon.

And I said, "Heracles! The man you speak of is not to be withstood, if only he happens to have one little thing besides."[8]

"What?" said Critias.

e   "If in respect to his soul," I said, "he happens to be of a good nature. Surely it is fitting, Critias, for him to be such, since he is of your family."

"But," he said, "he is quite a gentleman[9] in this respect too."

"Why, then," I said, "don't we strip this part of him and contemplate *it* before contemplating his looks? For surely at his age he is now quite willing to converse."

"Quite so," said Critias, "especially since he is both
155a   philosophic and, in the opinion of others as well as his own, quite poetic."

"This beautiful quality,[10] my dear Critias," I said, "is yours from far back, from your kinship with Solon.[11] But why

7. "Looks" translates *eidos* (also at 154d) and *idea* (157d, 158b, 175d). The meaning of these terms is "what something looks like." They are the words used by Plato in those dialogues that present his "theory of forms" or "doctrine of ideas." In this more technical meaning, the terms mean "what something looks like when the mind's eye sees it for what it is." Charmides and his many admirers seem to confuse what he looks like on the outside with what he looks like within.

8. Heracles, the legendary hero and warrior who performed the twelve labors, was one of the tutelary gods of wrestling-schools and wrestling. An oath by Heracles is a very manly exclamation. "Man" is *anēr*, an adult male, a surprising word to be applied to Charmides, who has just been called "lad" and "youth."

9. The Greek formula for "gentleman" is *kalos kai agathos*, literally "beautiful/ noble and good." This expression is often used of members of the old aristocratic families.

10. "This beautiful quality" is "this *kalon*," i.e., "this beautiful/noble/splendid (thing)." See n. 4 on *kalon*.

11. Solon was a famous Athenian statesman and poet of the late sixth century B.C. Although of noble birth himself, Solon reformed the polity by

don't you call the youth over here and show him to me? For
even if he happened to be still younger, surely it would not be
shameful for him to converse with us in front of you who are
at once his guardian and cousin."

"Beautifully spoken,"[12] he said; "we'll call him." And to
his attendant he said, "Boy, call Charmides and tell him I wish   b
to introduce him to a doctor in connection with that illness
from which he told me recently he was suffering." To me, in
turn, Critias said, "Lately he did say he has been somewhat
heavy in the head when he gets up in the morning. What
prevents you from pretending to him that you have knowledge of some drug for the head?"

"Nothing," I said. "Just let him come."

"He will come," he said.

And that is just what happened. For he came and
produced much laughter. For each of us who was seated,   c
making room so that he might sit beside him, was earnestly
shoving his neighbor, until we made the one sitting on one end
stand up and pushed the one on the other end off sideways.
But Charmides came and sat down between me and Critias.

Then indeed, my friend, I was in perplexity, and my
former boldness, which I had as I was expecting to converse
with him quite easily, had been knocked out of me. For when,
as Critias was saying that I was the one who had knowledge
of the drug, he looked at me with his eyes in such an
irresistible way and was drawing himself up to ask a   d
question, while everyone in the wrestling school flowed
around us in a complete circle—then indeed, O noble one, I
saw inside his cloak, I was inflamed, I was no longer in

abolishing serfdom, by dividing the citizenry into four classes based on wealth
rather than descent, and by granting to the common people some political
authority. ("Yours" and "your" in this sentence are plural—referring to both
Critias and Charmides—as is "your [family]" above at 154e.)

12. "Beautifully spoken" is a Greek idiom meaning "Well said," "What you say
is splendid," or "You've hit the nail on the head" (Critias is not praising Socrates'
pretty words).

Socrates knows he is out of his mind

control of myself, and I held Cydias[13] to be wisest in erotic matters, who, speaking about a beautiful boy, advised someone that "a fawn coming opposite a lion should beware lest he
e   be taken as a portion of meat." I myself seemed to myself to have been caught by such a creature. Nevertheless, when he asked me if I had knowledge of the drug for the head, with difficulty I somehow answered that I had knowledge of it.

"What is it, then?" he said.

And I said that it was a certain leaf, but that there was a certain incantation in addition to the drug, and that if one chanted it at the same time as he used it, the drug would make him altogether healthy, but without the incantation there would be no benefit from the leaf.

156a   And he said, "Then I'll write down the incantation from you."

"If you persuade me?" I said, "or even if you don't?"

So he laughed and said, "If I persuade you, Socrates."

"Well, then," I said. "And do you have my name precisely?"

"If I'm not doing an injustice," he said. "For there is no little talk about you among those of our age, and as for me even as a boy I remember your associating with Critias here."

"Beautifully done," I said. "I will speak more frankly to
b   you about the incantation, what sort it happens to be. Just now I was perplexed about how I might show you its power. For it is such, Charmides, that it does not have the power to make the head alone healthy. Just as you too perhaps have

---

13. The poet Cydias is otherwise unknown. "I was no longer in control of myself" is literally "I was no longer in my own."

Socrates is describing here an example of his own "sound-mindedness" or "moderation" in the sense of self-control of the bodily passions. But he may be exaggerating Charmides' effect on himself, perhaps with a view to the unnamed companion to whom he is narrating the dialogue. Socrates addresses the companion directly twice in this paragraph (and only once elsewhere: "comrade," at 154b). Consider Alcibiades' drunken testimony on Socrates' immunity to the physical attraction of beautiful young men in *Symposium* 216c–219e.

already heard from good doctors, whenever someone comes to them with his eyes in pain—they undoubtedly say that it is impossible to attempt to doctor the eyes alone, but it is necessary at the same time to treat the head as well, if the condition of the eyes is going to be good; so also they say it is quite mindless to suppose that one could ever treat the head itself by itself without the whole body. Because of this argument they turn to the whole body with their regimens and attempt to treat and doctor the part along with the whole. Haven't you noticed that they say this and that it is so?" c

"Quite," he said.

"Then is it beautifully spoken in your opinion, and do you accept the argument?"

"More than anything," he said.

And I, when I heard his praise, was again emboldened, and little by little my boldness rose back and I was rekindled to life. And I said, "Such also, then, Charmides, is how it is with this incantation. I learned it there in the army from one of the Thracian doctors of Zalmoxis, who, it is said, even immortalize people.[14] This Thracian said that Greek doctors say beautifully what I was just now saying. 'But,' he said, 'Zalmoxis, our king, who is a god, says that just as one must not attempt to doctor eyes without head or head without body, so also not body without soul; and that the cause of many diseases eluding the doctors among the Greeks is that d

e

---

14. Potidaea, where the Athenian army was, is not far from Thrace. According to Herodotus (IV 94-96), Zalmoxis is the god of the Getae, a tribe on the border of Thrace and Scythia (near the mouth of the Danube). Every five years, he says, the Getae "immortalize" (the same unusual word as here, but without the prefix: [ap]athanatizein) a man by tossing him into the air and letting him fall upon their spear points, after giving him messages for the god. Herodotus reports a story that Zalmoxis was in fact a Thracian slave of the philosopher Pythagoras who persuaded the people of his (and their own) immortality by disappearing into a secret underground chamber, and reappearing alive three years later. But Zalmoxis' doctors and their charms seem to be Socrates' (or Plato's) invention.

they are ignorant of the whole,[15] to which care must be given, because if *it* is not in beautiful condition, the part is not able to be in good condition. For he said that everything starts from the soul, both bad and good things for the body and for the entire human being, and they flow from there just as from the head to the eyes, and so one ought first and foremost to treat that, if the head and the rest of the body are going to be in beautiful condition.[16] He said that the soul is treated, blessed one, with certain incantations, and that these incantations are beautiful speeches; that from such speeches sound-mindedness comes to be in souls, and once it has come to be and is present, then it is easy to provide health both for the head and for the rest of the body.'

b   "So he taught me both the drug and the incantations and said, 'Let no one persuade you to treat his head with this drug unless he first submits his soul to be treated by you with the incantation. For as it is now,' he said, 'this is the error common among human beings, that some attempt to be doctors of these things separately, sound-mindedness and health.' And he commanded me quite vigorously to allow no

c one, however rich, noble, or beautiful, to persuade me to do otherwise. So I—for I swore an oath to him, and it is necessary for me to obey—will obey him. As for you, if you wish—in accordance with the commands of the foreigner—first to submit your soul to chant the incantations of the Thracian, I will apply the drug to your head. But if not, we would have nothing that we could do for you, my dear Charmides."

15. Burnet's text has "careless of the whole" here, but "ignorant of the whole" is the reading best supported by the manuscripts. This reading is especially plausible because it anticipates the later discussion of sound-mindedness as a knowledge of knowledge and of ignorance.

16. Note that if head is to eyes as soul is to body, and as whole is to part, then the body is part of the soul! If so, *all* diseases would be "psychosomatic." The Greek doctors, who distinguish soul from body, seem more sensible than the Thracians. Apparently Socrates adopts this dubious Thracian premise as a pretext for examining Charmides' soul.

When Critias heard me saying this, he said, "Socrates, the illness of the head would be a godsend for the youth[17] if he will be compelled because of his head to become better also in his thought. I say to you, however, that Charmides is reputed to be distinguished from those of his age not only in his looks but also in this very thing for which you say you have the incantation. You say it is for sound-mindedness, don't you?" "Quite so," I said.

"Then know well," he said, "that he is reputed to be quite the most sound-minded by far of his contemporaries; and in all other respects, to the extent he has reached maturity, he is second to none."

"Yes," I said, "and it is also just, Charmides, for you to be distinguished from others in everything of this sort. For I don't suppose that anyone else here would easily be able to show two such families—from the likely ones in Athens—that in uniting could give birth to someone more beautiful and better than those from which you were born. For your father's family, that of Critias son of Dropides, extolled by Anacreon,[18] by Solon, and by many other poets, has been handed down to us as distinguished in beauty and virtue, and in the rest of what is called happiness. And your mother's, in turn, is just the same. For no one on the continent is said to have been reputed to be superior to your uncle Pyrilampes in beauty or stature, on the many occasions when he went as an ambassador to the Great King[19] or to anyone else of those on the continent. This whole family is in no way inferior to the other.

"Since you are born from such as these, of course you are likely to be first in everything. So in regard to your visible

17. "Godsend" translates *hermaion*, a lucky find; after Hermes, the god of acquisition and good fortune.

18. This Critias was the grandfather of the Critias in the dialogue (*Timaeus* 20e). Anacreon was a famous lyric poet of the sixth century B.C.

19. The Great King: so the Greeks called the king of Persia, the principal power in Asia. He was proverbial for his wealth and ostentation. The "continent" is Asia.

b   looks, my dear son of Glaucon, in my opinion you bring shame
on none of your forebears.[20] And if your nature *is* sufficient in
sound-mindedness and in other respects, in accordance with
his statement, then, my dear Charmides," I said, "blessed did
your mother bear you.[21]

"So this is how it is: if sound-mindedness is already
present in you, as Critias here says, and you are sufficiently
sound-minded, you would no longer need the incantations
either of Zalmoxis or of Abaris the Hyperborean,[22] and the
c   drug for the head should be given to you now. But if you still
seem to be in need of these incantations, you must chant
before the giving of the drug. So tell me yourself whether you
agree with *him* and say that you already have a sufficient
share of sound-mindedness, or that you are in need."

𝒯

Blushing, Charmides first appeared even more beautiful—for
a sense of shame suited his age—and then he also answered in

20. This is the only manuscript reading that makes sense in the context. A
generally more reliable manuscript says, "in every respect you surpass none of
your predecessors." The editors Burnet and Croiset print "in every respect you are
less than none of your predecessors"; this plausible reading requires a conjectural
change of three letters in the manuscript. Note that the strange expression "visible
looks" implies that Charmides has "invisible looks," a possible allusion to his
"form" in the Platonic technical sense. See n. 7 on "looks."

21. This is probably an adaptation of Homer, *Odyssey* III 95, where Telemachus, seeking news of his father Odysseus, says of him to Nestor: "For, beyond
all, miserable did his mother bear him." Socrates' extravagant praise of the family
of Critias and Charmides must be taken with a grain of salt. The rest of the
dialogue, which exposes the deficiency of Charmides and then Critias, shows that
sound-mindedness by no means automatically comes with aristocratic ancestry.

22. In Herodotus' history (IV 32–36) the story of Abaris—he is said to have
carried an arrow around the world without stopping to eat—is the least
believable tale told about the mythical Hyperboreans ("people beyond the

no ignoble way. He said that it was unreasonable[23] under present circumstances either to agree with or deny what was asked. "For if," he said, "I say that I am not sound-minded, not only is it strange for one to say such things against oneself, but besides, I will give the lie to Critias here and many others, in whose opinion I am sound-minded, as he was saying. But again, if I say I am and praise myself, perhaps it will appear onerous. So I cannot answer you."

And I said, "What you say appears likely to me, Charmides. And in my opinion," I said, "we should investigate together whether or not you have acquired what I am asking about, so that you are not compelled to say what you don't wish to, and I do not turn to my doctoring without investigation. So if you like, I am willing to investigate along with you, but if not, to let it go."

"But I would like to," he said, "more than anything. So far as that's concerned, in whatever way you suppose the investigation is better, investigate in that way."

"Then in my opinion," I said, "we may best investigate it in this way. It is clear that if sound-mindedness is present to you, you can offer some opinion about it. For surely it is necessary that it, being in you, if it is in you, furnish some perception from which you have some opinion about it as to what and what sort of thing sound-mindedness is. Don't you suppose so?"

"I do suppose so," he said.

"Then as to that which you suppose," I said, "because you do have knowledge of how to speak Greek, you could also tell, no doubt, what it appears to you to be?"

"Perhaps," he said.

d

e

159a

North"), whose existence is attested only by poets and worshippers of Apollo on Delos. Nothing is said in Herodotus of any incantations.

23. "Unreasonable" (alogon) is in two manuscripts, including the best; the others have "not easy," preferred by most editors. Charmides' shame and silence here (alogon is literally "speechless") anticipate Critias' at 169c: in both cases concern for how one looks gets in the way of the argument (logos).

"So that we may get some notion, then, whether it is in
you or not," I said, "tell us what you say sound-mindedness is
in your opinion."

b   And at first he hesitated and wasn't quite willing to
answer. But then he said that in his opinion sound-mindedness was doing everything decorously and quietly, not only
while walking in the streets and conversing, but doing everything else in the same way. "And in my opinion," he said, "it is
in sum a certain quietness that you are asking about."[24]

"So," I said, "is that well said? To be sure, they do say,
Charmides, that the quiet are sound-minded. Let us see if there
c   is something in what they say. Tell me, isn't sound-mindedness assuredly among the beautiful things?"

"Quite so," he said.

"So which is most beautiful at the writing teacher's, to
write similar letters swiftly or quietly?"[25]

"Swiftly."

"What about reading? Swiftly or slowly?"

"Swiftly."

"And further, are playing the cithara swiftly and
wrestling keenly much more beautiful than doing so quietly
and slowly?"

"Yes."

"And what about boxing and the *pankration*?[26] Isn't it
the same?"

24. Charmides gives here a common sense definition of *sōphrosynē*. He
emphasizes the "moderation" or "self-control" aspect of the term. Our translation
"sound-mindedness" misses this sense somewhat. (See Introduction, on *sōphrosynē*.)

25. *hēsychēi*: quietly, gently, or slowly. The word translated "beautiful" here
and elsewhere is *kalon* (n. 4); in the present context its meaning is closer to
"splendid" or "fine." Again, we translate the term consistently because a major
question of the dialogue is whether that which is beautiful in its form (what looks
attractive on the surface) is also good. One instance of the question is whether the
beautiful Charmides and well-reputed Critias are sound-minded. Another is
whether the humble sound-mindedness discussed after 167a is also beneficial.

26. The *pankration* (literally, "all-strength") combined wrestling and boxing

"Quite so."

"And running and jumping and all the works of the body—aren't those beautiful that are done keenly and swiftly, d and those ugly that are done slowly, with difficulty, and quietly?"[27]

"It appears so."

"Then it is apparent to us," I said, "at least with regard to the body, that not what is quiet but what is swiftest and keenest is most beautiful, isn't it?"

"Quite so."

"But sound-mindedness was something beautiful?"

"Yes."

"Then at least with regard to the body, not quietness but swiftness would be more sound-minded, since sound-mindedness is something beautiful."

"It's likely," he said.

"What then?" I said. "Is learning well more beautiful or e learning poorly?"

"Learning well."

"And is learning well," I said, "to learn swiftly, while learning poorly is to do so quietly and slowly?"

"Yes."

"And isn't it more beautiful to teach someone swiftly and vigorously rather than quietly and slowly?"

"Yes."

"What then? Is it more beautiful to recollect and remember quietly and slowly or vigorously and swiftly?"

"Vigorously," he said, "and swiftly."

"Isn't readiness of mind a certain keenness, not quiet- 160a ness, of the soul?"

"True."

in an all-out contest of strength. The cithera in Socrates' previous question is an ancient guitar-like stringed instrument.

27. The word translated "ugly" is also the Greek word for "shameful"; it is the opposite of *kalon*.

"And so to comprehend what is said at the writing teacher's, at the citharist's, and everywhere else, not as quietly as possible, but as swiftly as possible, is most beautiful?"

"Yes."

"Moreover, in the soul's inquiries and in taking counsel it isn't the quietest one, I suppose, and he who takes counsel and makes discoveries with difficulty, who is reputed

b to be worthy of praise, but he who does this most easily and most swiftly."

"This is so," he said.

"So in all things, Charmides," I said, "both those concerning the soul and those concerning the body, don't those done swiftly and keenly appear more beautiful to us than those done slowly and quietly?"

"Probably," he said.

"Then sound-mindedness would not be a certain quietness, nor would the sound-minded life be quiet, at least from this argument,[28] since it must be beautiful if it is sound-minded. For it is one or the other of two things. Either

c nowhere or, if at all, in very few places did quiet actions in life appear more beautiful to us than swift and fierce ones. But even if, my friend, no fewer quiet actions happen to be more beautiful than are vigorous and swift ones, not even in this way would sound-mindedness be acting quietly rather than vigorously and swiftly, not in walking or speaking or anywhere else at all; nor would the quiet life, a decorous one, be

d more sound-minded than the one that is not quiet, because it was laid down in our argument that sound-mindedness is one

28. There are several obvious difficulties in Socrates' argument, and he may mean to allude to them with this qualification. Socrates' greatest "blunder" is to assume that if sound-mindedness is beautiful, anything beautiful must be sound-minded. There may be many beautiful things—Charmides himself, for example, or other virtues—that are not sound-minded. One should also remember that Socrates in all his doings proceeds quietly and slowly, never swiftly and vigorously. (Compare his calmness at the dialogue's beginning with the agitation of Chaerephon and Charmides' lovers.) Nor can the *Charmides* be read quickly if it is to be read well. *quietness has to do with body, not the mind*

of the beautiful things, and swift things have appeared no less beautiful than quiet ones."

"In my opinion, Socrates," he said, "you have spoken correctly."

"Back again, then, Charmides," I said, "apply your mind more and look into yourself: think over what sort of person sound-mindedness, by being present, makes you, and what sort of thing it is that would produce someone like that; and reckoning all this together, say well and courageously what it appears to you to be."

e

And after he paused and quite courageously investigated it thoroughly with regard to himself, he said, "Then in my opinion sound-mindedness makes a human being have a sense of shame and be ashamed, and sound-mindedness is just what respectfulness is."[29]

"Well, then," I said. "Weren't you just agreeing that sound-mindedness is something beautiful?"

"Quite so," he said.

"Then are the sound-minded also good men?"

"Yes."

"So would that which produces men who are not good be a good?"

"Of course not."

"So then it is not only something beautiful but also good."

"Yes, in my opinion."

161a

"What then?" I said. "Don't you trust that Homer speaks beautifully when he says, 'Respectfulness is not good for a needy man'?"[30]

---

29. *aidōs*: respectfulness, reverence, awe, and so a proper sense of shame or modesty before that which is conventionally reputed to be respectable or sacred. Charmides' first definition, "a certain quietness," is referred to the merely external appearance of moderation/sound-mindedness. His second, "respectfulness," goes deeper because it tries to specify the internal state of the moderate/sound-minded man.

30. *Odyssey* XVII 347. Telemachus, son of Odysseus, speaks these words to

"I do," he said.

"Then respectfulness, it seems, is a non-good and a good."

"It appears so."

"But sound-mindedness is a good, if it does make those to whom it is present good and not bad."

"Yes, in my opinion it does stand as you say."

b "Then sound-mindedness would not be respectfulness, if it does happen to be the good while respectfulness is something no more good than bad."

"Yes, in my opinion, Socrates," he said, "this is correctly spoken. But investigate this statement about sound-mindedness, what it is in your opinion. For I just recollected what I once heard someone say, that doing one's own things would be sound-mindedness. So investigate whether in your opinion he who says this speaks correctly."

And I said, "Wretch![31] You have heard it from Critias c here or from another one of the wise."

"Likely from another," said Critias; "certainly not from me."

"But what difference does it make, Socrates," said Charmides, "from whom I heard it?"

"None," I said. "For it must not at all be investigated who said it, but whether or not what is said is true."

"Now you're speaking correctly," he said.

"Yes, by Zeus," I said. "But if we do discover how it is, I would be surprised. For it looks like a kind of riddle."

his father when Odysseus returns to his home disguised as a beggar after a twenty-year absence. Telemachus means that Odysseus must put himself forward boldly and not be shy and deferential toward the high-born gentlemen who are occupying his house if he is not to come away empty-handed.

31. Wretch: *miaros*, literally "defiled with blood," "abominable." By using this harsh address, even in play, Socrates begins to shift the tone of the dialogue from the easygoing and attractive earlier part (dominated by the beautiful Charmides and the spirit of love) to the more spirited and combative part to follow (dominated by the honor-loving Critias).

"Because of what?" he said.

"Because," I said, "surely his words didn't express   d
what he had in mind when he said that doing one's own
things[32] is sound-mindedness. Or do *you* believe the writing
teacher does nothing when he writes or reads?"

"I certainly don't believe so," he said.

"So in your opinion does the writing teacher write and
read only his own name and teach you boys to do so, or did
you write your enemies' no less than your own and your
friends' names?"

"No less."

"So you were being meddlesome and not sound-
minded when doing this?"   e

"In no way."

"And yet you were not doing your *very* own things, if
writing and reading are 'doing something.' "

"But they are."

"And further, comrade, doctoring and housebuilding
and weaving and producing by any art at all any of the works
of an art—surely these are 'doing something.' "

"Quite so."

"What then?" I said. "In your opinion would a city be
well managed under a law that bids each one to weave and
wash his own cloak, and to cobble his shoes and his oil flask
and scraper[33] and everything else according to the same
account: that he not touch the things of another, but that each   162a
produce and do his own things?"

"Not in my opinion," he said.

32. "Doing one's own (things)" literally translates "*to ta heautou prattein,*"
normally meaning "minding one's own business," "not being meddlesome."
Socrates defines justice as "doing one's own things" in *Republic* 433a, where it
means doing that work well in the city for which one is best suited by nature, and
443d, where it means ordering the parts of the soul properly, with the intelligent
part ruling the others.

33. When the Greeks bathed, they oiled themselves and afterwards scraped
their skin.

"But being managed sound-mindedly," I said, "it would be managed well."

"How not?" he said.

"Then," I said, "doing such things as these and doing one's own things in this way would not be sound-mindedness."

"It appears not."

"Then, it seems, he was speaking in riddles, as I was just saying, when he said that doing one's own things is sound-mindedness. For surely he wasn't so simple as that. Or
b did you hear someone foolish say this, Charmides?"

"Least of all," he said, "as he was reputed to be *quite* wise."

"Then more than anything, in my opinion, he put it forward as a riddle, being aware that it is hard to recognize[34] whatever doing one's own things is."

"Perhaps," he said.

"So whatever would doing one's own things be? Can you say?"

"*I* don't know,[35] by Zeus!" he said. "But perhaps nothing prevents even the one who said it from not knowing what he had in mind." And while he was saying this, he laughed slightly and looked at Critias.

Ⅱ

---

34. *Gignōskein* will be translated "recognize" (the negative, *agnoein*, "be ignorant") to distinguish it from *epistasthai* ("have knowledge") and *eidenai* ("know"). *Gignōskein*, one of the three main "know" verbs used in the dialogue, has the sense of "come to know" or "realize," while the other two are "know" in the stative sense of already possessing knowledge. Related nouns are *gnōrimos*, "acquaintance" (153a and c), and *gnōsis*, "cognition" (169e).

35. "Know" is *eidenai*. The second "know" system derives from "see," and its root sense is "to have seen"; that is, once one has perceived something, one knows it. The word "know" will be exclusively reserved for *eidenai*, "have knowledge" for *epistasthai*. See nn. 34 and 46.

And it had long been clear that Critias was anxious to c
contend and win honor before both Charmides and those
present; and having held himself back with difficulty earlier,
he now became unable to. In my opinion what I suspected is
more true than anything, that Charmides had heard this
answer about sound-mindedness from Critias. Now Charmides, not wishing himself to give an account of the answer
but for Critias to, kept prodding him and pointing out that he d
had been refuted. But he didn't endure this, and it was my
opinion that Critias was angry with him, just as a poet is with
an actor who recites his poems badly. So he looked at him and
said, "Do you suppose, Charmides, that if you don't know
what he had in mind who said that sound-mindedness is
doing one's own things, therefore he doesn't know either?"

"But Critias, best of men," I said, "it's no wonder that
he at his age is ignorant. But you, no doubt, are likely to know e
because of your age and the care you have taken. So if you
concede that sound-mindedness is what he says and take over
the argument, I would be much more pleased to investigate
with you whether or not what was said is true."

"But I quite concede it and take it over," he said.

"Beautifully done, then," I said. "Now tell me, do you
also concede what I was just now asking, that all craftsmen
make something?"[36]

"I do."

"So is it your opinion that they make only their own 163a
things or also those of others?"

"Also those of others."

"So are they sound-minded in not making only their
own things?"

"What prevents it?" he said.

"Nothing on my part," I said. "But see whether it
doesn't prevent him who, after setting down that doing one's

36. Socrates had in fact spoken of artisans *doing*, not *making* something
(161e). See the next note.

own things is sound-mindedness, then asserts that nothing
prevents also those who do the things of others from being
sound-minded."

"I, no doubt," he said, "have agreed that those who do
the things of others are sound-minded if I agreed that those
who make them are."[37]

b   "Tell me," I said, "don't you call making and doing the
same?"

"Certainly not," he said. "Nor working and making.
For I learned from Hesiod, who said that 'work is no disgrace.'[38] So do you suppose, if he was calling such works as
you were just now speaking of both working and doing, that
he would say that it wasn't a disgrace for someone to be a
shoemaker or salt-fish seller or prostitute? One ought not to
suppose so, Socrates; but he too, I suppose, held that making
is something other than doing and working, and that although

c   a thing made sometimes becomes a disgrace—whenever it
doesn't come into being along with that which is beautiful—a
work is never a disgrace at all. For things made beautifully
and beneficially he called works, and such makings he called
workings and doings. One ought to say that he believed that

37. Probably spoken with sarcasm. In this section "make" will translate
poiein, "do" prattein. (Exception for prattein: at 160c, "actions" and "acting" are
used.) The Greeks often use poiein, like the German machen, as an equivalent of
"do." Poiein is often so translated elsewhere (e.g. "beautifully done," 162e, and the
three "doings" at 166c).

38. Works and Days 311. Hesiod's authority in antiquity rivaled Homer's. In
Hesiod's poem, work (ergon) means primarily farming, in Critias' view a suitable
occupation for an aristocratic gentleman. Critias has an aristocratic disdain for
ordinary artisans—for whatever is not kalon, i.e., beautiful or impressive to the
outward view. Xenophon reports that Socrates was accused of teaching his
companions to be tyrants by interpreting this line of Hesiod to mean that one
should do anything, however unjust or shameful, for the sake of gain. In response,
Xenophon says that Socrates "said those who make something good are 'working'
and 'workers,' while gamblers and those who make anything else that is worthless
and leads to loss he called idlers" (Memorabilia I 2.56–57). Here and elsewhere
Critias may be repeating things he has heard Socrates say—putting his own twist
on them, of course.

only such as these are kindred to oneself,[39] while everything harmful is alien. Therefore, one ought to suppose that Hesiod and anyone else who is prudent call the one who does his own things sound-minded."

"Critias," I said, "right away, even as you were begin- d ning, I almost understood your argument: that you call things good that are kindred to oneself and one's own, and you call the makings of good things doings. For I have heard Prodicus[40] too drawing some ten thousand distinctions among names. I give you leave to set down each of the names however you wish, but only make clear to what you are referring whatever name you say. So now back again, define it more plainly from the beginning. The doing of good things, or making, or however you wish to name it—is this what you say sound- e mindedness is?"

"I do," he said.

"Then he who does bad things is not sound-minded, but he who does good things is?"

"In your opinion, best of men," he said, "isn't it so?"

"Let that go," I said. "For let us not yet investigate what my opinion is, but what you are saying now."

"But I do assert," he said, "that he who makes not good but bad things is not sound-minded, whereas he who makes good but not bad things is sound-minded. For I plainly define for you that the doing of good things is sound-mindedness."

"And nothing, perhaps, prevents you from speaking 164a the truth. However, I do wonder about this," I said, "whether

39. "Kindred to oneself" is oikeion, an expression for "one's own" that is related to oikia, translated "family" at 157e–158a and "household" at 171e and 172d. Critias seems to mean that one should embrace whatever benefits oneself as "kindred" or "one's own." But he understands "beneficial" as "beautiful," i.e., splendid or noble—reflecting well on oneself. Thus Critias rejects shoemaking as disgraceful even though shoes are beneficial in a humble way.

40. The sophist Prodicus was highly reputed for his expertise in grammar and philology, and he stressed the need for precision in the use of words (Protagoras 339e–341c). "Name" is the Greek term for "word."

you believe that human beings who are sound-minded are ignorant of being sound-minded."

"I don't believe this," he said.

"A little earlier," I said, "wasn't it said by you that nothing prevents craftsmen, even when they make the things of others, from being sound-minded?"

"Yes, that was said," he said. "But what of it?"

"Nothing. But say whether in your opinion a certain
b doctor who makes someone healthy makes beneficial things both for himself and for him whom he doctors?"

"In my opinion he does."

"Now doesn't he who does this do what is needed?"

"Yes."

"Isn't he who does what is needed sound-minded?"

"He certainly is sound-minded."

"So is it necessary for the doctor also to recognize when he is doctoring beneficially and when not? And for each of the craftsmen to recognize when he is going to profit from the work that he is doing and when not?"

"Perhaps not."

"Then sometimes," I said, "the doctor who has done
c something beneficially or harmfully does not recognize how he himself did it.[41] And yet having done it beneficially, as your argument has it, he did it sound-mindedly. Weren't you saying so?"

"I was."

"As it seems, then, sometimes he who does something beneficially does it sound-mindedly and is sound-minded, but is ignorant of being sound-minded himself?"

"This, Socrates," he said, "would never happen. But if you suppose that something I agreed to earlier necessarily

41. The Greek idiom literally means "does not recognize himself—how he did it." Socrates employs this idiom here and in his next question ("is ignorant of himself—that he is sound-minded") to introduce the theme of "self-knowledge." (Compare 164a where it is not used.)

leads to this conclusion, *I* would rather put one of those things aside, and I wouldn't be ashamed to say that I haven't spoken   d
correctly rather than ever concede that a human being who himself is ignorant of himself is sound-minded.

"For *I* assert that this is almost what sound-mindedness is: recognizing oneself; and I go along with the one who put up such an inscription at Delphi.[42] For this inscription in my opinion was put up as if it were a greeting of the god to those entering, instead of 'hail,' in the view that this greeting, 'hail,' is not correct, and that they should not exhort each other   e
to this, but to be sound-minded. Thus the god addresses those entering the temple somewhat differently than do human beings. Such was the thinking of the one who put it up when he put it up, in my opinion. And he says to whoever enters nothing other than 'be sound-minded,' he asserts.[43] He says it, of course, in a rather riddlesome way, like a diviner. For 'know yourself' and 'be sound-minded' are the same, as the inscription and I assert. Yet someone might perhaps suppose   165a
they are different, which is what happened in my opinion to those who put up the later inscriptions 'Nothing too much' and 'A pledge, and bane is near.'[44] For they supposed that 'Know yourself' is a counsel, not a greeting by the god for the sake of

---

42. The reference is to the famous inscription at the Delphic oracle of Apollo, *gnōthi seauton*, "Know yourself" (or "Recognize yourself").

43. "He says...he asserts": Presumably the first "he" refers to the god, the second to the one who put up the inscription. If we generalize from Critias' story here, our beliefs about the gods come from sayings made up by a few men who pretend that the gods said them.

44. The proverb "Nothing too much" might well stand as the popular definition of moderation/sound-mindedness. Strikingly, Critias completely rejects this definition.

"A pledge, and bane is near": that is, if you act as guarantor for someone, he may default, leaving you liable for the debt. The Delphic inscriptions "Know yourself" and "Nothing too much" were popular and often quoted (*Protagoras* 343b).

those entering. And then, so that they too might put up
counsels no less useful, they wrote these and put them up.[45]
    "Why I am saying all this, Socrates, is this. Everything
b earlier I am taking back for you. For perhaps in some way you
were speaking more correctly about them, perhaps I was, but
nothing of what we were saying was quite plain. But now I
am willing to give you an account of this, if you don't agree
that sound-mindedness is oneself recognizing oneself."
    "But Critias," I said, "you are coming at me as though I
claim to know what I am asking about and would agree with
you if only I should wish to. But that is not how it is, for I am
inquiring along with you into whatever is put forward
c because I myself don't know. So after I investigate I am
willing to say whether I agree or not, but wait until I
investigate."
    "Investigate, then," he said.
    "I am investigating," I said. "For if sound-mindedness
is recognizing something, it is clear that it would be a kind of
knowledge,[46] and one that is *of* something, or wouldn't it?"
    "It is," he said, "namely of oneself."
    "And isn't also doctoring," I said, "a knowledge, of the
healthful?"
    "Quite so."

---

45. Critias' point here seems to be that gods do not give counsels (moral
advice, as if to inferiors) but rather greetings (as if to equals). He implies that the
author of the inscription "Know yourself" meant that the gods, and the wise who
understand their hints, are beyond good and evil. They do not impose moral
limits on human beings. (The moralistic view of the gods comes in with the
second generation of inscribers.) Thus moderation/sound-mindedness is the
amoral "recognize yourself"—know what you are doing and whether you will
benefit from it—not the restraining counsel "nothing too much."

46. "Knowledge" will always be a translation of *epistēmē*; "have knowledge"
(never "know") will translate the related verb *epistasthai*. (See nn. 34 and 35 on
the other two "know" verbs.) We revive below a venerable usage of the word
"knowledge" in the plural, which for centuries was often employed to designate
the different branches of learning, as we use the term "sciences" today.

"If, then," I said, "you should ask me, 'if doctoring is a knowledge of the healthful, in what respect is it useful for us and what does it produce?' I would say, 'no little benefit; for it produces health, a beautiful work for us,' if you accept this."   d

"I accept it."

"And if, then, you should ask me, 'if housebuilding is a knowledge of building houses, what work do I say it produces?' I would say 'houses.' And the same with the other arts. So since you assert that sound-mindedness is a knowledge of oneself, you ought to be able to speak on its behalf when you are asked, 'Critias, if sound-mindedness is a knowledge of oneself, what beautiful work for us does it produce worthy of   e its name?' Come now, speak."

"But, Socrates," he said, "you are not inquiring correctly. For this is not similar in its nature to the other knowledges, nor are the others to each other. But you are making the inquiry as though they are similar. For tell me," he said, "what work is there from the art of calculation or geometry such as a house from housebuilding or a cloak from weaving or other such works, many of which one could show from many arts? So can you in turn show me some such work   166a from these? But you won't be able to."

And I said, "What you say is true. But I can show you what each of these knowledges is a knowledge of, which happens to be other than the knowledge itself. Thus calculation, surely, is of the even and odd in regard to multitude, in their relations to themselves and to each other, isn't it?"

"Quite so," he said.

"So are the odd and the even different from calculation itself?"

"How not?"

"And again, the weighing of the heavier and the   b lighter measure is weighing, and the heavy and light are different from weighing itself. Do you concede it?"

"I do."

"Say, then, what is sound-mindedness also a knowledge of which happens to be different from sound-mindedness itself?"

"This is it, Socrates," he said. "You have come in your search to the very thing by which sound-mindedness differs from all the knowledges, yet you are inquiring after some similarity between it and the others. But this is not how it is; rather, while all the others are knowledges of something else and not of themselves, it alone is a knowledge both of the other knowledges, and itself of itself. And you are far from being unaware of this, for you are doing, I suppose, what you just denied that you were doing. You are attempting to refute me and letting go of what the argument is about."

"What a thing you are doing!" I said, "by believing, even if I *do* refute you, that I am refuting for the sake of anything other than that for the sake of which I would also search through myself as to what I say, fearing that unawares I might ever suppose that I know something when I don't know. So I do assert that this is what I am also doing now: investigating the argument most of all for the sake of myself, but perhaps also for my other companions. Or don't you suppose that it is a common good for almost all human beings that each thing that exists should become clearly apparent just as it is?"

"I do very much, Socrates," he said.

"Then be bold, blessed one," I said, "and answer however what is asked appears to you, letting go of whether Critias or Socrates is the one being refuted. But apply your mind to the argument and investigate in what way it will turn out under refutation."[47]

"Yes, I will do so," he said, "for in my opinion you speak with due measure."

---

47. With these remarks Socrates finally gets Critias to give up his contentiousness and stick to the argument. Thus is established the tone of the rest of the dialogue (dominated by the philosophic Socrates) up to the conclusion: it is highly intellectual, impersonal, abstract—and, at least on the surface, less attractive. Cf. n. 31.

"Say, then," I said, "what are you saying about sound-mindedness?"

"I say, then," he said, "that it alone of the other knowledges is a knowledge both of itself and of the other knowledges."

"So wouldn't it be," I said, "a knowledge also of non-knowledge, if it is also of knowledge?"[48]

"Quite so," he said.

"Then only the sound-minded one will himself both 167a recognize himself and be able to examine both what he happens to know and what he does not; in the same way it will be possible for him to investigate others in regard to what someone knows and supposes, if he does know, and what he himself supposes he knows but does not know.[49] No one else will be able to. And this is what being sound-minded, and sound-mindedness, and oneself recognizing oneself are: knowing both what one knows and what one does not know. Is this what you are saying?"

"I am," he said.

48. Socrates' little addition to Critias' definition points to the decisive difference between the two men. Critias emphasizes knowing one's powers and abilities, in accordance with his earlier concern for elegant profit (163c). But Socrates shifts the focus to knowing one's limits, since he is far less confident than Critias that he knows what is truly profitable for him. Critias' complacent self-assurance leads him to seek honor for what he is, while Socrates' knowledge of his non-knowledge impels him to seek the knowledge he knows he lacks.

49. "And what he himself supposes he knows" is the reading of all the manuscripts. Burnet and others change this to read "and again, what he [i.e., someone else] supposes he knows." Apparently the editors are disturbed by Socrates' sudden shift from examining others to examining oneself, since he had seemed to conclude his statement on examining oneself earlier in the sentence.

What Socrates describes here as sound-mindedness seems to be identical to the "human wisdom" which is the only wisdom claimed by him in the *Apology* (20d).

Back again, then," I said. " 'The third one for the Savior.' As if
b from the beginning let us investigate first whether it is
possible for this to be or not—to know what one knows and
what one does not know, that one does not know it—and next,
even if it is possible, what benefit there would be for us in
knowing it."[50]

"Yes, that ought to be investigated," he said.

"Come then, Critias," I said, "investigate whether you
appear any more resourceful than I about this. For I am
perplexed. Shall I tell you in what way I am perplexed?"

"Yes, do," he said.

"If what you were just now saying is so," I said, "then
wouldn't all this be one kind of knowledge which is a
c knowledge of nothing other than itself and the other knowledges, this same one being in particular a knowledge of non-
knowledge as well?"

"Quite so."

"See what a strange thing we are attempting to say,
comrade. For surely if you investigate this same thing in other
things, it will seem to you, I suppose, to be impossible."

"How and where?"

"In these. Think over whether in your opinion there is
a kind of seeing that is not a seeing of what the other seeings
are of, but is a seeing of itself and of the other seeings, and in
d the same way of non-seeings: one which, although it is a
seeing, sees no color, but sees itself and the other seeings. In
your opinion is there such a one?"

"No, by Zeus, not in mine!"[51]

---

50. At banquets the third of three libations was offered to Zeus the Savior;
apparently this final round was regarded as especially propitious (Republic 583b,
Laws 692a).

The two questions posed here and the object of the rest of the dialogue: is this
knowledge possible, and if so, is it beneficial? See the outline at the end of the
Introduction.

51. Critias cannot understand that such self-related activities of the soul are
possible. Yet he himself experiences such a seeing without recognizing it. At 168e

"What about a hearing that hears no sound, but hears itself and the other hearings and non-hearings?"

"Not this, either."

"In sum, investigate concerning all perceptions whether in your opinion there is a kind of perception of perceptions and of itself that perceives nothing of what the other perceptions perceive."

"Not in mine."

"But is there in your opinion a kind of desire that is a e desire of no pleasure, but is of itself and of the other desires?"

"Of course not."

"Nor a wish, I suppose, that wishes nothing good, but wishes itself and the other wishes."

"Certainly not."

"Would you assert that there is a kind of erotic love such that it happens to be a love of nothing beautiful, but is of itself and of the other loves?"

"Not I," he said.

"Have you ever noticed a kind of fear that fears itself and the other fears, but fears not even one of the terrible 168a things?"

"I haven't noticed one," he said.[52]

"Or an opinion that is an opinion of opinions and of itself, but which opines nothing of what the others opine?"

"In no way."

"But, it seems, we assert that there is a kind of knowledge such that it is a knowledge of nothing learned, but is a knowledge of itself and of the other knowleges."

"Yes, we do assert it."

"So it is a strange thing, if it turns out that there is? Let us not yet strongly affirm that there is not, but let us investigate further whether there is."

he sees that something appears impossible to him; in other words, he sees with his "mind's eye" a seeing (or a non-seeing) of his "mind's eye." So there is a kind of seeing that sees itself and other seeings but sees no color.

52. Roosevelt did: "The only thing we have to fear is fear itself."

b   "What you say is correct."
         "Come then. This knowlege is a knowledge of some-
thing, and it has a kind of power so that it is *of* something,
doesn't it?"
         "Quite so."
         "For we assert that the greater also has a kind of
power so that it is greater *than* something."[53]
         "Yes, it has."
         "Than something less, then, if it is going to be
greater?"
         "Necessarily."
         "So if we should discover something greater that is
greater than the greater things and than itself but is not
greater than any of the things that the other things are greater
c than, then surely it would altogether be in the situation that if
it *was* greater than itself it would also be less than itself,
wouldn't it?"
         "Most necessarily, Socrates," he said.
         "So also if there is a kind of double of the other
doubles and of itself, doubtless it would be a double of itself
(which would be a half) and of the others, wouldn't it? For
surely a double is not double of anything other than a half."
         "True."
         "Won't what is more than itself also be less, and what
is heavier, lighter, and what is older, younger? And in the
d same way with everything else, won't whatever has its own
power with regard to itself also have that being with regard to
which its power is? I'm speaking of something of this sort.
Hearing, we say, wasn't a hearing of anything other than of
sound; isn't this so?"
         "Yes."

53. In Greek "of something" (Socrates' previous question) and "than something" are both expressed by the genitive *tinos*. Hence there is no transition from
"of" to "than" in Greek. Note that in the following *quantitative* relations (unlike
the soul-relations just discussed) the self-relation that Socrates is looking for is
truly impossible.

"So if it is going to hear itself, it will hear itself by having a sound. For otherwise it wouldn't hear."

"Most necessarily."

"And surely seeing, best of men, if it is going to see itself, will itself necessarily have some color. For seeing would never see anything colorless."   e

"No, it wouldn't."

"So you see, Critias, that of the things we have gone through, some of them appear altogether impossible to us, while we vigorously distrust that the others would ever have their own power with regard to themselves? For as to sizes and quantities and such like, it is altogether impossible, isn't it?"

"Quite so."

"However, hearing and seeing, again, and further, a motion itself moving itself, and a heat kindling, and again, all such things, might afford distrust to some, but perhaps not to   169a certain others. Some great man, my friend, is needed, who will draw this distinction capably in everything: whether none of the things that are has itself by nature its own power with regard to itself, except knowledge, but has it with regard to something else, or whether some have it and others don't; and again, if there are some things that themselves have it with regard to themselves, whether among them is a knowledge that we assert is sound-mindedness.[54]

"Now I don't trust myself to be capable of drawing these distinctions. Therefore I can also neither strongly affirm whether it is possible for this to come to be—for there to be a   b knowledge of knowledge—nor, even if it is possible, do I accept that it is sound-mindedness, until I investigate whether something that is of this sort would benefit us or not. For I do

54. Socrates is asking: can something (seeing or knowing) have its own power (sight or knowledge) with regard to itself? Can seeing see itself? Can knowing know itself?

divine that sound-mindedness *is* something beneficial and good.

"So you, son of Callaeschrus[55]—for you set it down that sound-mindedness is a knowledge of knowledge and particularly of non-knowledge—show first that it is possible for you to demonstrate what I was just saying, and then, in addition to being possible, that it is also beneficial. Then c perhaps you would satisfy me too that you are speaking correctly about what sound-mindedness is."

When Critias heard this and saw me in perplexity, then, just as those who see people yawning right across from them have the same happen to them, so he too in my opinion was compelled by my perplexity and was caught by perplexity himself. Now since he is well-reputed on every occasion, he was ashamed before those present, and he was neither willing to concede to me that he was unable to draw the distinctions I called upon him to make, nor did he say d anything plain, concealing his perplexity.

And I, so that our argument might go forward, said, "But if it seems proper,[56] Critias, let us concede for now that it is possible for a knowledge of knowledge to come to be. Some other time we will investigate whether or not this is so. So come then, even if this *is* possible, how is one any more able to know both what one knows and what not? For this surely was what we were saying was to recognize oneself and to be sound-minded, weren't we?"

"Quite so," he said, "and surely that *is* the conclusion, e Socrates. For if someone has a knowledge that itself recognizes itself, he himself would be of the same sort as what he has. Just as when someone has swiftness he is swift, and when beauty he is beautiful, and when cognition he is

---

55. The name Callaeschrus means something like "Ugly Beauty" or "Shameful Nobility."

56. This expression *(ei dokei)* may also mean "if it is so resolved," as if by a political assembly.

cognizant, so also when someone has cognition itself of itself, surely he will then be cognizant himself of himself."

"It is not this," I said, "that I dispute—that whenever someone has that which is cognizant of itself, he himself will recognize himself—but this: what necessity is there for him who has this to know both what he knows and what he does not know?"

"Because, Socrates, this is the same as that?[57]   170a

"Perhaps," I said, "but probably I am always like this. For again I don't understand how knowing what one knows and knowing what someone does not know are the same."[58]

"What are you saying?" he said.

"This," I said. "If there is a knowledge of knowledge, will it be able to distinguish anything more than this: that this one of these is a knowledge and that one is not a knowledge?"

"No, but just so much."

"So are knowledge and non-knowledge of the healthful, and knowledge and non-knowledge of the just, the   b same?"[59]

57. Critias may mean: "Knowing what one knows and doesn't know is the same as having that which is cognizant of itself." But he could mean: "Knowing what one knows is the same as knowing what one doesn't know." This section is very abstract (there are no "he said's" or personal addresses from 170a6 to 171c9) and difficult, especially in these first few exchanges. Bruell and Tuckey (see Bibliography) have made some sense of it.

58. Socrates' most obvious meaning is: "I don't understand how knowing what one knows is the same as knowing what someone does not know." But in light of his following explanatory remark, the present statement would mean: "I don't understand how knowing what one knows and doesn't know is the same as having that which is cognizant of itself." Thus the question of knowledge of *non*-knowledge in particular, which seemed to be raised here, gets skirted (as Socrates points out at 175c), although it casts its shadow on what follows.

59. In light of Socrates' next remark, this question seems to mean: "Are knowledge and non-knowledge of the healthful the same as knowledge and non-knowledge of the just (or the same as a knowledge of knowledge)?" The point made by Socrates in the remarks that follow is that a knowledge of knowledge won't be able to distinguish doctoring from politics—or from a knowledge of knowledge!—because *all* it knows is that each is a knowledge. Likewise a

"In no way."

"One, I suppose, is doctoring, one is politics, and one is nothing other than knowledge."

"How not?"

"So if someone does not have knowledge in addition of the healthful and the just, but recognizes only knowledge (as he has a knowledge only of this), then it is likely that he would recognize that he has knowledge of something and that he has a kind of knowledge, both concerning himself and conerning others, isn't it?"

"Yes."

c   "But how will he know by this knowledge *that* he recognizes? For he recognizes the healthful by doctoring, not by sound-mindedness; harmonics by music, not by sound-mindedness; and housebuilding by housebuilding, not by sound-mindedness; and so on in everything. Isn't it so?"

"It appears so."

"But if sound-mindedness *is* a knowledge only of knowledges, how will he know by it that he recognizes the healthful or housebuilding?"

"He will in no way."

"Then he who is ignorant of this will not know *what* he knows but only *that* he knows."

"It is likely."

d   "Then being sound-minded, and sound-mindedness, would not be knowing both what one knows and what one does not know, but only, it seems, that one knows and that one does not know."

"Probably."

"Nor, then, will he be able to examine whether another claiming to have knowledge of something does have knowledge or doesn't have knowledge of what he says he has knowledge of. Rather, he will recognize only this much, it

knowledge of non-knowledge won't distinguish non-knowledge of justice from non-knowledge of the healthful.

seems: that he has a kind of knowledge. But sound-minded-ness will not make him recognize what it is of."

"It appears not."

"Then he won't be able to judge between one who   e
pretends to be a doctor but is not and one who truly is, nor between any others of those who have knowledge and those who don't. Let us investigate it from the following. If the sound-minded one, or anyone else at all, is going to recognize one who truly is a doctor and one who isn't, he won't do it like this: surely he won't converse with him about doctoring. For the doctor has no expertise, as we were saying, except in the healthful and the diseaseful, does he?"

"Yes, that is so."

"About knowledge he knows nothing; we assigned this to sound-mindedness."

"Yes."

"Then the skilled doctor doesn't know about doctoring either, since doctoring does happen to be a knowledge."   171a

"True."

"The sound-minded one will recognize *that* the doctor has a kind of knowledge; but if one needs to try to grasp *what* it is, will he investigate anything other than what it is of? Or isn't it in this respect that each knowledge has been defined not only to be a knowledge but also which one it is: in its being *of* certain things?"

"In this respect, certainly."

"And doctoring was defined as being different from the other knowledges in its being a knowledge of the healthful and diseaseful."

"Yes."

"So it is necessary for him who wishes to investigate doctoring to investigate it in whatever it is involved in. For   b
doubtless not in what is outside of it, at least, in which it is not involved?"

"Of course not."

"Then he who investigates correctly will investigate

the doctor, in respect to his being a skilled doctor, in what is healthful and diseaseful—"

"Likely."

"—by investigating in what is spoken or done in a certain way whether what is spoken is truly spoken and what is done is correctly done?"

"Necessarily."

"So would someone without doctoring be able to follow either of these?"

"Of course not."

c   "Nor yet would anyone else, it seems, except a doctor, and certainly not the sound-minded one. For he would be a doctor in addition to his sound-mindedness."

"That is so."

"More than anything, then, if sound-mindedness is only a knowledge of knowledge and of non-knowledge, it will not be able to judge between a doctor who has knowledge of the things of his art and one who does not have knowledge but pretends or supposes he does, nor anyone else of those who have knowledge of anything at all, except for the one with the same art as himself, as is the case with other craftsmen."[60]

"It appears so," he said.

d   "Then what benefit, Critias," I said, "would still come to us from sound-mindedness if it is such as this? For if, as we were setting it down from the beginning, the sound-minded one knows both what he knows and what he doesn't know— that he knows the one and that he doesn't know the other— and if he were able to investigate someone else in this same state, it would be grandly beneficial to us, we assert, to be sound-minded. For we would live through life without error, we ourselves and those who have sound-mindedness, and all
e   others who were ruled by us. For we ourselves would not

60 Sound-mindedness (knowledge of knowledge and non-knowledge) can recognize the presence or absence of knowledge. But since it is ignorant of the content, it cannot recognize whether someone is an expert or a pretender in any particular art. Only a doctor—someone who has learned what makes people healthy and sick—can reliably distinguish a doctor from a quack.

attempt to do what we didn't have knowledge of, but we would find those who had knowledge and hand it over to them. And to others whom we ruled we would not turn over anything to be done except what they would do correctly when they did it; and this would be what they had a knowledge of. And a household managed by sound-mindedness would be beautifully managed, as would a city so governed, and everything else that sound-mindedness would rule. For with error taken away and correctness leading, it is   172a necessary for those so situated to do beautifully and well in every doing, and for those who do well to be happy. Isn't this, Critias," I said, "what we were saying about sound-mindedness, when we said how much of a good it would be to know both what someone knows and what he does not know?"

"It certainly is," he said.

"But as it is now," I said, "do you see that no such knowledge has appeared anywhere?"

"I see," he said.

"So," I said, "does what we are now discovering   b sound-mindedness to be—having knowledge of knowledge and non-knowledge—have this good: that he who has it will learn more easily whatever else he learns and that everything will appear more distinct to him, since in addition to each thing he learns, he will also discern the knowledge? And that he will examine others more beautifully about whatever he himself has learned, while those who examine without this will do it more weakly and poorly? Is it such things as these, my friend, that we will enjoy from sound-mindedness? And   c are *we* looking at something greater and requiring it to be something greater than it is?"[61]

61. Sound-mindedness (knowledge of knowledge and of non-knowledge) would after all have some benefit. It is a precondition of examining oneself and others and facilitates all learning. But progress will be arduous and slow, since the examiner of oneself and others must also learn in each case—to the extent it can be learned—the subject matter on which he examines a pretender to knowledge. This must be how Socrates proceeds. Such a way of life no doubt

"Maybe," he said, "that is so."

"Perhaps," I said. "And perhaps *we* inquired into nothing useful. I take as evidence that certain strange things about sound-mindedness are becoming clearly apparent to me if it is such as this. Let us see, if you wish, by conceding that we know it is possible even to have knowledge of knowledge; and let us not strip away but let us grant what we were setting down sound-mindedness to be from the beginning: knowing both what one knows and what one does not know.

d   And granting all this, let us investigate still better whether if it is such as this it will then also be of any profit to us. For as to what we were saying just now—how great a good sound-mindedness would be if it is such as this, leading the management of both household and city—in my opinion, Critias, we have not agreed beautifully."

"How?" he asked.

"Because," I said, "we easily agreed that it is some great good for human beings if each of us does what he knows and hands over what he does not have knowledge of to others who have knowledge."

e   "So didn't we agree beautifully?" he said.

"Not in my opinion," I said.

"What you say is truly strange, Socrates," he said.

"Yes, by the dog!"[62] I said, "that is my opinion too, if I said that when I looked at it then and just now, strange things were becoming apparent to me and I feared we were not investigating correctly. For truly, even if sound-mindedness *is*

173a such a thing, it is not clear in my opinion that it produces a good for us."

---

strikes Critias as paltry and ugly next to the beautiful shortcut to happiness sketched by Socrates in his picture of a utopia run by experts. (The word translated "requiring" in this sentence and "inquired" in the next is the same verb, *zētein*.)

62. "By the dog" is an oath apparently unique to Socrates. He swears "by the dog, the Egyptians' god" at *Gorgias* 482b; "the dog" may be Anubis, the mediator between the upper and lower world, whose Greek counterpart is Hermes.

"How?" he said. "Speak, so that we too may know what you are saying."

"I suppose," I said, "that I am babbling. Nevertheless, it is necessary to investigate just what appears and not to pass by indifferently if one is concerned for oneself even a little."

"Yes, that is beautifully spoken," he said.

"Then hear my dream," I said, "whether it came through horns or through ivory.⁶³ Even if sound-mindedness *would* rule us, it being such as we now define it, would everything be done in any other way than in accordance with the knowledges? Someone claiming to be a pilot, but who is not, would not deceive us, nor would we be unaware of a doctor or a general or anyone else pretending to know something that he doesn't know. From this being so, would there be any other conclusion for us than that we would be healthy in our bodies more than now, that those endangered at sea and in war would survive more, and that equipment, clothing, all footwear, and all our possessions would be produced for us more artfully, and much else as well, because of our using true craftsmen? If you wish, let us concede that divination too is a knowledge of what is going to be, and that sound-mindedness, presiding over it,⁶⁴ will turn away the boasters and establish for us true diviners, prophets of what is to be. That the human kind, so equipped, would act and live knowledgeably, I can follow, for sound-mindedness being on guard would not allow non-knowledge to creep in and be our fellow-worker. But that in acting knowledgeably we would do well and be happy—this we are not yet able to learn, my dear Critias."

b

c

d

---

63. Homer, *Odyssey* XIX 564-567: "Those dreams that come through the gate of sawn ivory deceive, bringing words which are unfulfilled; but those that come through the gate of polished horn fulfill true things, when any mortal sees them." These are the gates of the underworld.

64. "Preside over," *epistatein*, has the same root as *epistēmē*, "knowledge," and so creates a pun. Similarly at 174d-e.

"But," he said, "you will certainly not easily find some other delimitation of 'doing well' if you dishonor 'knowledgeably.' "

"Then teach me," I said, "yet a little thing in addition. Of what are you saying 'knowledgeably'? Shoemaking?"

e   "No, by Zeus, not I!"

"Or working with bronze?"

"In no way."

"Or with wool or wood or anything else of that sort?"

"Of course not."

"Then no longer," I said, "are we abiding by the argument that he who lives knowledgeably is happy. For although these live knowledgeably, they are not agreed by you to be happy. But in my opinion the happy man is defined well as one of those who live knowledgeably.[65] And perhaps you are saying it is the one I just now spoke of, he who knows

174a everything that is going to be, the diviner. Are you saying that it is he or someone else?"

"I say both he," he said, "and another."

"Who?" I said. "Someone of the sort who might know, besides what is to be, also everything that has happened and what is now, and be ignorant of nothing? Let us set down that someone of this sort exists. I don't suppose you would say there is anyone who lives still more knowledgeably than he."

"Of course not."

"This is what I am still longing for in addition: which of the knowledges makes him happy? All of them alike?"

"In no way alike," he said.

b   "But which one in particular? The knowledge by which he knows *what* among what is and what has happened and what is going to be? The one by which he knows draught-playing?"

---

65. Burnet and Croiset, changing the manuscripts' *zōntōn eu dokei* to *zōnta su dokeis*, read "but in my opinion you define the happy man as the one who lives knowledgeably about certain things."

"Draught-playing!" he said.

"By which he knows calculation?"

"In no way."

"By which he knows the healthful?"

"More so," he said.

"But the one that I particularly speak of," I said, "is that by which he knows what?"

"That by which he knows the good and the bad," he said.

"Wretch!" I said. "You have been dragging me around in a circle, concealing that it was not living knowledgeably that makes one do well and be happy, not even if it be with all the other knowledges together, but with one alone, of the good and bad. Because, Critias, if you are willing to take this knowledge away from the other knowledges, will doctoring make one any less healthy, or will piloting any the less prevent one from dying at sea, or generalship in war?"

"No less," he said.

"But, my dear Critias, we will be deprived of having each of these done well and beneficially if this knowledge is absent."

"What you say is true."

"This one, at any rate, it seems, is not sound-mindedness, but one whose work is to benefit us. For it is the knowledge not of knowledges and of non-knowledges, but of good and bad. So if this one is beneficial, sound-mindedness would be something other than beneficial to us."

"Why," he said, "wouldn't it be beneficial? For even if sound-mindedness is a knowledge of knowledges, it also presides over the other knowledges, and, no doubt, since it would rule this knowledge about the good, it would benefit us."

"Would it also make someone healthy," I said, "rather than doctoring? And would it make the other products of the arts too, rather than each of the others making its own product? Or weren't we long bearing witness that it is a

knowledge only of knowledge and of non-knowledge but of
nothing else? Isn't it so?"

"It appears so, at least."

"Then it will not be a craftsman of health."

"Of course not."

175a
"For health was from another art, wasn't it?"

"From another."

"Then it is also not a craftsman of benefit, comrade.
For again, we gave this work away to another art just now,
didn't we?"

"Quite so."

"How then will sound-mindedness be beneficial if it is
a craftsman of no benefit?"

"In no way, Socrates, at least as is likely."

"So do you see, Critias, that my fear was a likely one
all along, and that I was justly accusing myself of investigating nothing useful about sound-mindedness? For surely

b   what is agreed to be most beautiful of all would not have
appeared unbeneficial to us if I had been of any benefit with
regard to inquiring beautifully. For as it is now, we are
everywhere worsted, and we are unable to discover which-
ever of the things that are that the lawgiver set this name
upon, 'sound-mindedness.'[66]

"And yet we have conceded much that cannot be
concluded from our argument. For we conceded that there is a
knowledge of knowledge, although the argument did not
allow or declare that there is. And again, we conceded to this
knowledge that it also recognizes the works of the other

c   knowledges, although the argument did not allow that either,
so that our sound-minded one might become knowledgeable
of both what he knows, that he knows it, and of what he does
not know, that he does not know it. This we conceded

66. The notion that words were made up by a "lawgiver" according to a
rational plan is the hypothesis of the *Cratylus*, where it is carried to a comic
extreme.

altogether magnificently, not even investigating the impossibility of someone somehow or other knowing what he does not know at all. For our agreement asserts that he knows that he does not know this. And yet, as I suppose, nothing would appear more unreasonable than this. But although the inquiry has found us so simple and unstubborn, nevertheless it is no   d
more able to discover the truth. Rather, it laughed at the truth so much that it was quite hubristically making apparent to us that what we were long agreeing to and fabricating together and setting down to be sound-mindedness, is unbeneficial.
"Now for myself I am less annoyed. But for you, Charmides," I said, "I am quite annoyed, if you, being such as you are in your looks and besides this most sound-minded in your soul, won't profit from this sound-mindedness and if it,   e
being present, won't be of any benefit to you in your life. I am still more annoyed over the incantation I learned from the Thracian, if, when it was for a matter of no worth, I was learning it with such earnestness.
"So this I certainly do not suppose is so, but rather that I am a poor inquirer, and that since sound-mindedness is some great good, if you do have it, you are blessed. But see whether you have it and are not in need of the incantation. For   176a
if you have it, I would counsel you rather to believe that I am a babbler and unable to inquire by argument into anything at all, and that you yourself, so far as you are more sound-minded, are also that much happier."
And Charmides said, "But by Zeus, Socrates, I don't know whether I have it or don't have it. For how would I know what not even you two are able to discover—namely, what ever it is—as you yourself say? I however don't quite   b
believe[67] you, and, Socrates, I suppose myself to be quite in need of the incantation. And for my part, at least, nothing

67. "Believe" is the same verb (peithesthai) translated "obey" at 176c. In the active voice the verb means "persuade" (156a).

prevents it from being chanted by you for as many days as it takes until *you* say it is sufficient."

"Well, then," said Critias. "But, Charmides, if you do this, it will be evidence, at least for me, that you are sound-minded, if you submit to Socrates to chant and don't abandon him either much or little."

"You can count on me to follow," he said, "and not c abandon him. For I would be doing something terrible if I wouldn't obey you, my guardian, and do what you bid be."

"But I do bid you," he said.

"Then I shall do so," he said, "beginning from this very day."

"Hey," I said, "what are you two taking counsel to do?"

"Nothing," said Charmides; "we *have* taken counsel."

"Then will you use violence," I said, "and not even grant me a preliminary inquiry?"[68]

"You can count on me to use violence," he said, "since *he* is ordering me to. You, in turn, take counsel as to what you will do in view of this."

d "But no counsel is left," I said. "For if you attempt to do anything at all, especially by violence, no human being will be able to oppose you."

"No, then," he said, "don't *you* oppose either."

"No, then," I said, "I won't oppose."

---

68. The magistrate who was to preside over a jury trial would conduct a preliminary inquiry in which both parties presented statements and evidence before the trial. Socrates playfully implies that Charmides' (the "you" here is singular) headstrong insistence on having his own way is potentially lawless. By concluding the dialogue with talk of violence, Plato reminds his readers of Charmides' fate as a major figure in Critias' violent tyranny in whose overthrow the two men died violently in turn. Socrates had also alluded to Charmides' potential for violence earlier, at 156a.